SCOTCH WHISKY

by

George For'

£6 95

Published in Scotland in 1995 by Lang Syne Publishers Ltd.
Clydeway Centre, 45 Finnieston Street, Glasgow G3 8JU
and printed by Dave Barr Print.
Origination by Newtext Composition Ltd,
© LANG SYNE PUBLISHERS Ltd. 1995.
Much of the material in Chapters One to Six is
reproduced by kind permission of The Scotch Whisky Association.
This material is © The Scotch Whisky Association.

ISBN: 1 85217 007 7

Contents

CHAPTER ONE

Introduction

FEW modern industries can trace their roots back five hundred years but thanks to a medieval monk the Scotch Whisky industry can do just that.

For it was in 1494 that Friar John Corr recorded in the Scottish Exchequer Rolls "eight bolls of malt wherewith to make aquavitae" (the latter meaning 'water of life' in Gaelic and the traditional description of whisky). This was equivalent to more than a ton of malted barley, sufficient to produce 1400 bottles of spirits, so obviously distilling was a well established practice in religious houses where the beneficial, tonic effects of whisky were quickly recognised. This note is also the first recorded instance of excise duty on whisky so tax and drink went hand in hand from the beginning.

Nowadays Scotch whisky is sold in 190 markets worldwide (the French drink more of it than brandy).

It is consistently one of Britain's top five export earning industries, generating two billion pounds of overseas sales annually.

There are 22 bottles sold overseas every second.

Almost 80 million cases are sold each year.

Whisky is the only truly international drink and is also extremely versatile and can be drunk in all sorts of mixtures.

Exports account for 85% of sales.

The industry contributes a billion pounds each year to the British Government in taxes.

There are 15,000 people employed in Britain directly in the industry and they support up to four jobs each among suppliers and distributors. It is also vital to many rural areas devoid of any other industry and to areas of high unemployment where many blending and bottling halls are located.

Whisky is almost symbolic of the enterprising Scot himself - ebullient, original, versatile, international with a quality, grace and style, a consistency, history and heritage unique to the product of the the mountains and the glens.

Here then is all you wanted to know about Scotland's national drink and a few unusual facts you may not have come across before.

We start by going back into the Scotch mists of history....

Enjoying a taste of the water of life

CHAPTER TWO

The History of Scotch Whisky

L IKE most things, distilling is believed to have originated with the ancient Egyptians and there is evidence that it was practised as long ago as 800 BC.

The art may have been brought to Scotland by Christian missionary monks and the ancient Celts were the first to call the fiery liquid produced from surplus barley 'uisge beatha' or the water of life.

To the natives of Caledonia in their frozen forests and bleak moors its startling ability to revive cold bodies and warm the blood was indeed a gift of the gods.

The earliest reference to a distillery in the Acts of the Scottish Parliament appears to be in 1690 when mention is made of the famous Ferintosh distillery owned by Duncan Forbes of Culloden.

There is also reference to distilling in a private house in the parish of Gamrie in Banffshire in 1614. This appears in the Register of the Privy Council where a man was accused of the crime of breaking into a private house and assault and knocking over some aquavitie.

A mention of 'uiskie' is made in the funeral account of a Highland laird in 1618 and in 1622 Sir Duncan Campbell of Glenorchy wrote to the Earl of Mar that officers sent by the King had been given the best entertainment that the season and the country allowed and went on 'for they wantit not for wine nor aquavitie'.

Distillation methods improved and in the 16th and 17th centuries considerable advances were made.

The dissolution of the monasteries contributed to this since many of the monks driven out onto the open road had no choice but to put their distilling skills to good use and this knowledge spread among the general populace, many of whom were keen to cash in on this new innovation.

Whisky, as it came to be coloquially known, was lauded for its medicinal qualities and was prescribed for the relief of colic, palsy, smallpox and other

Rolling out the barrel circa 1900

ailments. It was also believed to prolong life.

James Hogg, the 'Ettrick Shepherd', penned the immortal lines on the same subject:-

"If a body could just find out the exact proper proportion and quantity that ought to be drunk every day, and keep to that, I verily trow that he might live forever, without dying at a', and that doctors and kirkyards would go oot o' fashion."

The spirit became an integral part of Scottish life and culture, toasted by Burns and Scott, and used as a social lubricant at weddings, funerals, parties and dances.

It kept the populace warm during long winter nights and was used as a traditional greeting to guests.

Taxation was never far away, however, and this increased with the Treaty of Union of 1707 when England set out to civilize the barbarous Scots.

Distilling was driven underground and a long battle of wits ensued between excisemen and illicit distillers. Frequently these cat and mouse games in the mountains and glens led to bloodshed.

Smuggling flourished round the coast for 150 years and sometimes it seemed as if the whole country was involved in scenes reminiscent of 'Whisky Galore' with the spirit being stowed in out-of-the-way places and

Workers at Glenmorangie Distillery pictured earlier this century.

the natives trying desperately to avoid the watchful eyes of the government officers.

By 1777 in Edinburgh eight licensed distilleries were contributing to the U.K. economy but 400 unregistered stills were being run by freebooters in the city. This meant there must have been thousands throughout the Highlands and Islands.

By the 1820s more than half the whisky consumed in Scotland was being made illegally despite the fact that 14,000 illicit stills were being closed down annually.

Eventually the Duke of Gordon pressed in the House of Lords for more distilleries to be granted legal licences.

In 1823 the Excise Act was passed which sanctioned the distilling of whisky in return for a licence fee of £10 and a set payment of 2/3d per gallon of proof spirit.

This was the beginning of the Scotch Whisky industry as we know it today.

Smuggling died out over the following decade and many of the present day distilleries stand on sites used by smugglers in the old days.

In 1831 Aeneas Coffey developed the Patent Still which enabled a continuous process of distillation to take place and this in turn led to the pro-

Cardhu Distillery workers in Speyside pictured during the late nineteenth century.

duction of grain whisky, a different, less intense spirit from the malt whisky produced in the copper pot stills.

The invention was exploited by Andrew Usher who in the 1860s blended malt and grain whiskies together for the first time to produce a lighter flavoured drink which extended the appeal to a broader public.

Around this time the industry received a boost from an unexpected quarter when the vineyards of France were decimated by disease and wine and brandy disappeared from world markets.

By the time the French products recovered, whisky had successfully established itself as a drink in polite society.

The grand but futile experiment of Prohibition introduced in America meant that when it was inevitably repealed in 1933 there were no producers of spirits in the United States and Scotch whisky had to be shipped over in bulk.

Following the end of the last war the British Government actively encouraged exports of whisky to bolster foreign exchange. Serving GIs returning home, who had discovered the delights of Scotch for themselves, were only too happy to help in this effort.

Scotch whisky has literally gone from strength to strength, improving in taste and quality over the years, and has survived the various ups and downs of history to maintain its position now as the beloved international alcoholic beverage.

CHAPTER THREE

How It Is Made

WHISKY can only be called Scotch Whisky if it is distilled and matured for at least three years in Scotland.

Distilleries are generally located in the most picturesque settings, close to the natural ingredients on which the industry depends.

There are two kinds of Scotch whisky - malt which is made by the pot still process and grain which is made by the patent still process.

Malt whisky is made from malted barley only.

Grain whisky is made from malted barley together with unmalted barley and other cereals.

Inside a modern distillery

A cooper hammers out metal strips for barrels

Malt whisky:-

The pot still process by which malt whisky is made may be divided into four main stages - malting, mashing, fermentation and distillation.

The barley is first screened to remove any foreign matter and then soaked for two to three days in tanks of water known as steeps.

After this it is spread out on a concrete floor known as the malting floor and allowed to germinate.

Germination may take from 8 to 12 days depending on the season of the year, the quality of the barley used and other factors.

During germination the barley secretes the enzym diastase which makes the starch in the barley soluble thus preparing it for conversion into sugar.

Throughout this period the barley must be turned at regular intervals to control the temperature and rate of germination.

At the appropriate moment germination is stopped by drying the malted barley or green malt in the malt kiln.

More usually nowadays malting is carried out in Saladin boxes or in drum maltings, in both of which the process is controlled mechanically.

Instead of germinating on the distillery floor, the grain is contained in large rectangular boxes (called Saladins) or in large cylindrical drums.

Temperature is controlled by blowing air at selected temperatures upwards through the germinating grain which is turned mechanically.

A recent development caused by the rapid expansion of the industry is for

Securing the barrels

distilleries to obtain their malt from centralised maltings which supply a number of distilleries thereby enabling the malting process to be carried out more economically.

The dried malt is ground in a mill and the grist, as it is now called, is mixed with hot water in a large circular vessel called a mash tun.

The soluble starch is thus converted into a sugary liquid known as wort. This is drawn off from the mash tun and the solids remaining are removed for use as cattle food.

After cooling, the wort is passed into large vessels holding anything from 9,000 to 45,000 litres of liquid where it is fermented by the addition of yeast.

The living yeast attacks the sugar in the wort and converts it into crude alcohol.

Fermentation takes about 48 hours and produces a liquid known as wash containing alcohol of low strength, some unfermentable matter and certain by-products of fermentation.

Malt whisky is distilled twice in large copper pot stills.

The liquid wash is heated to a point at which the alcohol becomes vapour. This rises up the still and is passed into the cooling plant where it is condensed into a liquid state.

The cooling plant may take the form of a coiled copper tube or worm that

Checking for quality

is kept in continuously running cold water or it may be another type of condenser.

The first distillation separates the alcohol from the fermented liquid and eliminates the residue of the yeast and unfermentable matter.

This distillate, known as low wines, is then passed into another still where it is distilled a second time.

The first runnings from this second distillation are not considered potable and it is only when the spirit reaches an acceptable standard that it is collected in the Spirit Receiver.

Again, towards the end of the distillation, the spirit begins to fall off in strength and quality.

It is then no longer collected as spirit but drawn off and kept, together with the first running, for redistillation with the next low wines.

Grain whisky -

This is made from malted barley mixed with unmalted barley together with wheat or maize.

The cereals are first cooked under pressure in order that their starches can be broken down into fermentable sugars.

Copper stills at work

The cereals can then be combined with a proportion of malted barley in the mash tun and mixed with boiling water to produce the sugary liquid known as wort.

The resultant wort is fermented to produce the wash which then passes into the massive, continuously operating, two-columned Coffey or Patent Still.

The skills of the stillman required to judge the moment at which malt and grain spirit is ready to be collected are crucial to the art of distilling.

Once the quality is approved, the malt and grain spirit is filled into casks of oak wood which allow air to pass in and evaporation to take place in cool, dark warehouses.

The harsher constituents are thus removed and the new spirit becomes in due course a mellow whisky.

Malt whisky, which contains more of these flavoury constituents, takes longer to mature than grain whisky and is often left in casks for 15 years or longer.

The quality of the casks is carefully monitored as the new spirit is to gain character and colour from the wood in which it rests. Some casks will previously have been used to hold oloroso, fino or amontillado sherries. Some

Another part of the distillation process

will have contained bourbon and some will be new oak. The type of cask used for maturation will have been determined by the Master Blender who is seeking a particular character and continuity for the whisky.

Far and away the greatest proportion of Scotch whisky is consumed in blended form.

The highly complex tasks of creating a marriage of single malt and single grain whiskies to make a blended whisky, and of maintaining the consistency of the blend, is the responsibility of the Master Blender.

The art of blending has been compared to conducting an orchestra. The individual players may be unique and brilliant in their own right, as are the single malt and grain whiskies, but someone has to ensure that the individual players harmonise.

The blender's aim is to produce a whisky which is different from others, a little more subtle, a little more complex than the individual whiskies which have gone into the blend.

A blend can be a judicious combination of anything from 15 to 50 single whiskies of varying ages compiled to a highly secret formula.

Inside the bottling plant

It is the Master Blender's nose which is the final judge of his creation and he will have spent long years mastering and perfecting the art of nosing. For this task he uses a tulip shaped glass.

Selection of the single whiskies is of the utmost significance. There are over 100 distilleries located in Scotland making malt or grain whisky and the blender will choose which products he requires as well as their different ages.

Most of his work is carried out in a blending room under very controlled conditions so that no other smell can interfere with his senses.

After he has checked them by nosing the contents of each cask, all of the whiskies are brought together in vats and then filled back into casks where they will rest for a further period of up to six or eight months.

This is known as 'the marriage' - the period during which each whisky harmonises with the others.

The blend is then reduced to the strength required by the addition of water.

The different whiskies in the blend will have derived some colour from the casks in which they have been matured and the degree of colour will vary from one whisky to another.

The whisky is then filtered carefully, bottled and packaged or shipped overseas in bulk.

Malt whiskies are divided into four groups according to the geographical location of the distilleries in which they are made - Lowland, Highland, Speyside and Islay.

The natural elements of water, peat and the Scottish climate have a magical effect on the flavour and effect of whisky.

Scottish water is famous for its purity and all distilleries are located near a stream or river which provides a good source of this basic liquid. The peat, used in the kiln or oven in which the malt is dried, can create a smoky flavour while the climate is vital during maturing with soft air permeating the casks to eliminate the harsher constituents thus ensuring a mellower drink.

Different locations is usually the reason given for the various distinctive flavours but one of the many delights of whisky is that the formula which ensures success is still shrouded in mystery even after so many centuries of manufacturing. Even some of those involved in vital tasks during the making cannot fully explain the workings of their various skills.

Many companies, particularly abroad, have tried to make synthetic whisky under artificial conditions but they have failed dismally, much to the delight of the Scots and the continuing health of their native industry.

CHAPTER FOUR

World Conquest

IF ANY product can be said to have conquered world markets it is sure-ly Scotch whisky, currently exported to more than 190 countries.

It is one of the top five export earning industries in Britain.

No other alcoholic drink can offer the individual taste and character of Scotch whisky produced from over a hundred different distilleries.

Although it has been legally produced on a large scale for more than 170 years, the international sales of whisky received a boost after the Second World War. To help earn badly needed foreign currency the industry organised a voluntary scheme for restricting releases of the drink to the home market. This lasted until 1954 but not until the early sixties did releases in Britain reach pre-war levels.

Since that time regular and severe increases in excise duty have artifi-cially restricted releases from bond warehouses which would reasonably have been expected to rise steadily with increasing prosperity.

Whisky earns large amounts of foreign currency each year and 85% of all sales are abroad.

Only between 15% and 20% of whisky sold in Britain is consumed in Scotland.

The major foreign markets are now the European community, the USA and Japan but with the dismantling of the Iron Curtain the formerly com-munist countries of Eastern Europe and Russia are now offering a new, expanding market as their fledgling democracies get under way.

If Britian is included, the EC accounts for more than half the total sales of whisky.

Current stocks of Scotch in this country stand at 2,543 million litres.

Stocks of mature and maturing whisky are now sufficient to cover pro-jected sales for almost nine years.

Ninety-five per cent of all Scotch whisky consumed is in blended form,

SCOTCH WHISKY AS AN EXPORT EARNER

THE TOP TEN MARKETS 1993

	VALUE	VOLUME*
USA	£282.5m	144.4m
FRANCE	£216.3m	108.3m
SPAIN	£188.0m	86.7m
JAPAN	£139.0m	58.0m
VENEZUELA	£ 83.6m	32.9m
GREECE	£ 82.8m	41.6m
THAILAND	£ 73.2m	20.8m
GERMANY	£ 69.3m	31.4m
ITALY	£ 59.5m	30.2m
PORTUGAL	£ 46.8m	22.4m

* 70cl Bottles

EXPORTS OVER THE LAST TEN YEARS

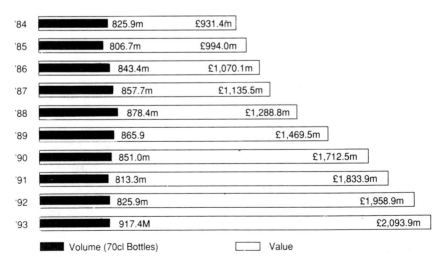

Year	Volume (70cl Bottles)	Value
'84	825.9m	£931.4m
'85	806.7m	£994.0m
'86	843.4m	£1,070.1m
'87	857.7m	£1,135.5m
'88	878.4m	£1,288.8m
'89	865.9	£1,469.5m
'90	851.0m	£1,712.5m
'91	813.3m	£1,833.9m
'92	825.9m	£1,958.9m
'93	917.4M	£2,093.9m

■ Volume (70cl Bottles)   ☐ Value

Bell's whisky being delivered to outlets in the USA.

enjoyed on its own or with water or soda or lemonade or other mixers or in a cocktail.

Traditionally sipped as an aperitif, it is drunk more and more through meals as a complement to food and is also increasingly enjoyed as a digestif.

Malt whisky is fast gaining popularity as an after drink of choice as opposed to brandy or liqueurs.

Traditionally the malts are sipped and savoured in a 'snifter' glass neat or with a touch of water.

There is a whisky to match every kind of weather and every mood at any time of the day or night.

More than two thousand brands are available worldwide and not one tastes the same as another.

It is eminently suitable to today's taste for drinking less but drinking better.

It is a natural product compatible with modern environmental concerns.

A measure of Scotch contains less calories than a half pint of regular beer or a glass of wine.

Pioneering sales to USA.

In moderation whisky can relieve stress and promote appetite and sleep, especially among the elderly.

For all these reasons it is in step with modern trends concerning alcohol consumption and looks set to remain a world leader into the foreseeable future.

You cannot beat quality.

Staff of William Grant's Distillery.

CHAPTER FIVE

Popular Drinks and Recipes

1. Scotch Tom Collins.
   5 - 6 dashes of lemon.
   1 large glass of Scotch.
   2 - 3 lumps of ice.
   Pour into a large glass and fill with soda.

2. Scotch Horse's Neck.
   Lemon juice.
   Angostura.
   Scotch.
   Ginger ale.

3. Whisper.
    2 glasses of Scotch.
    2 glasses of French vermouth.
    2 glasses of Italian vermouth.
    Cracked ice.

4. Clansman's coffee.
    1 oz. of Scotch.
    three quarters oz. Sambucca
    Black coffee.
    Whipped cream.

Wipe the rim of a goblet with a piece of lemon and dip it in brown sugar.
Pour the spirits and coffee into the glass, add sugar to taste and float the
whipped cream on top. Decorate with grated chocolate.

5. Scotch Fizz.
    1 oz. of Scotch.
    half an ounce of Fraise.
    Chilled champagne.

Pour the spirits into a wide champagne glass and top with champagne.
Decorate with a strawberry.

6. Green Mist.
    1 oz. of Scotch.
    1 oz. of creme de menthe.
    half an ounce of lemon juice.

Shake the ingredients, strain into a cocktail glass. Decorate with a slice of
kiwi and a sprig of mint.

7. Rob Roy.
    half Italian vermouth.
    half Scotch.
    Dash of angostura.

8. Highland Special.
    3 glasses of Scotch.
    2 glasses of French vermouth.
    half a glass of orange juice.
    Add a little nutmeg after mixing.

9. Summer Scotch.
   1 glass of Scotch.
   3 dashes of creme de menthe.
   1 lump of ice.
   Fill glass with soda.

10. Scotch Rickey.
    1 lump of ice.
    Juice of half a lime.
    Juice of a quarter of a lemon.
    1 glass of Scotch.
    Soda.

11. Derby Fizz.
    5 dashes of lemon juice.
    1 teaspoonful of powdered sugar.
    1 egg.
    3 dashes of Curacao.
    1 glass of Scotch.
    Soda water.

12. Highland Cooler.
    1 teaspoonful of powdered sugar.
    Juice of half a lemon.
    2 dashes of angostura.
    1 glass of Scotch.
    1 lump of ice.
    Ginger ale.

13. Earthquake.
    One third gin.
    One third Scotch.
    One third anis aperitif.

14. Flying Scotsman.
    Two and a half glasses of Italian vermouth.
    3 glasses of Scotch.
    1 tablespoonful of bitters.
    1 tablespoon of sugar syrup.

15. Scotch whisky toddy.
Place a spoonful of sugar in a warm glass and add enough boiling water to dissolve the sugar and hot lemon juice. Add a generous measure of Scotch and stir with a silver spoon; pour in more boiling water and top up with more whisky. Stir well.

16. Atholl Brose.
Mix an equal quantity of honey (preferably heather honey) and fine oatmeal in a little cold water. Add the Scotch and stir until frothy. Bottle and keep for two days before serving. Two pints of whisky will be needed for a half-pound of honey and a half-pound of oatmeal.

17. Whisky sour.
To a double Scotch add the juice of half a lemon and half a teaspoonful of sugar. Shake with ice and serve with a squirt of soda water.

18. Whisky Mac.
Scotch and green-ginger wine to taste. They may be in equal proportions or two thirds whisky and one third green-ginger wine.

19. Highland Fling.
    1 oz. of Scotch.
    1 oz. Amaretto.
    Ginger ale.
Mix in a long glass. Decorate with a twist of orange spiralling into the glass.

20. Purple Heather.
    1 measure of Scotch.
    1 teaspoon of Cassis.
    Ice.
Pour into a tall glass and top up with soda.

21. Bannockburn.
  1 glass of Scotch.
  1 dash of Worcestershire sauce.
  Tomato juice.
  1 slice of lemon.
  Ice.

22. Scotch Chicken.
  One and a half pounds of chicken.
  2 oz. butter.
  1 glass of Scotch.
  1 cup of fresh cream.
  Seasoning.
Cut the chicken in two and cook in melted butter for about 20 minutes. Add seasoning to taste. When cooked, remove chicken and keep it warm. Skim the fat and deglace the pan with the Scotch. Add cream to sauce and pour over chicken before serving.

23. Prince Charlie's Souffle.
  1 oz. butter.
  1 oz. flour.
  Quarter pint of milk.
  1 oz. castor sugar.
  2 tblsp. whisky liqueur.
  3 egg yolks.
  4 egg whites beaten.
  Fifteen and a half oz. can of raspberries.

24. Flora's whisky omelette.
  6 eggs.
  Half an ounce of butter.
  1 tblsp. sugar.
  2 tblsp. Scotch whisky.
  1 tblsp. Cointreau.
Separate egg yolks from whites. Whisk egg whites until still enough to stand in peaks. Whisk the yolks then whisk into the egg whites. Melt the

butter in a 9 - 10 inch frying pan and heat till foaming and just beginning to turn brown. Pour the mixture into the pan and spread out evenly. Cook over a medium heat till the underside is lightly brown, loosen edges with a knife, then place under a medium grill for 2 -3 minutes to brown lightly and to set the top. Quickly take to the table, sprinkle with sugar and pour mixed whisky and Curacao or Cointreau over the top and set alight.

CHAPTER SIX
Questions and Answers

What is the difference between Scotch, Irish, Rye and Bourbon whiskies?

Scotch whisky means whisky distilled and matured in Scotland.Irish whiskey means whiskey distilled and matured in Ireland. In Scotland whisky is distilled from malted barley in pot stills and from malted and unmalted barley with other cereals in patent stills.Irish whiskey is distilled using similar methods to those used in Scotland. As regards Bourbon, United States regulations state that Bourbon whiskey must be produced from a mash of not less than 51% corn grain and that Bourbon cannot describe any whiskey or whiskey-based distilled spirits not produced in the United States. Rye whiskey is produced both in the United States and Canada.In the USA Rye whiskey by definition must be produced from a grain mash of which not less than 51% is rye grain.

At what strength is whisky sold in the U.K. and for export?

All whisky is retailed at a minimum 40% volume of alcohol for the home market. A strength of 43% volume is often found in export markets.

Why is Scotch whisky so expensive in Britain?

Because taxation is extremely high, accounting for around 70% of the retail price of a bottle of standard blended whisky.

How does the rate of duty in the U.K. on Scotch whisky compare with that on other alcoholic drinks?

The Excise Duty paid on mature spirits is the same regardless of whether they are produced in this country or abroad. However, whisky is discriminated against when competing in the U.K. market against imported wines which are taxed at little more than half the rate borne by Scotch.

How many brands of Scotch whisky are there?

There are as many as two thousand brands sold around the world but it would be impossible to count every brand of Scotch whisky marketed. Many are sold only locally or to private clubs and individuals.

What are the best blends?

This is entirely a matter of taste. All whiskies produced nowadays are of good quality and meet high standards of excellence.

How is the expression 'the real McCoy' connected with Scotch?

Captain Bill McCoy, a Scottish skipper, used to smuggle real Scotch whisky into the USA during Prohibition hence the expression.

What was the most expensive bottle of Scotch sold?

It was a bottle of 50-year-old malt sold at a charity auction in Milan in 1992 for £47,000.

What is the percentage of malt and grain whiskies in blended Scotch?

There is no fixed percentage. The proportion differs from one blender to another.

What is de luxe blended Scotch whisky?

It is a blend which contains a higher proportion of carefully selected older and therefore more expensive whiskies.

When there is an age label on a bottle of blended whisky does it refer to the average age of the whiskies in that blend?

No. The law requires that when the age is declared on a label it must refer to the youngest whisky in the blend.

Is it legal to sell whisky which is less than three years old for consumption in this country?

No. Although the spirit is distilled under the strict conditions applied to the production of Scotch whisky, it is not entitled to be described as whisky until it has matured for three years.

What was meant by proof spirit?

The Customs and Excise Act of 1952 defined spirits of proof strength as follows:-'Spirits shall be deemed to be at proof if the volume of the ethyl alcohol contained therein made up to the volume of the spirits with distilled water has a weight equal to that of twelve-thirteenths of a volume of distilled water equal to the volume of the spirits, the volume of each liquid being computed as at fifty-one degrees Fahrenheit. 'In other words, proof spirit meant that the spirit at a temperature of 51 degrees Fahrenheit weighed exactly twelve-thirteenths of a volume of distilled water equal to the volume of the spirit. It was, in fact a mixture of spirit and water of a strength of 57.1% of spirit by volume and 42.9% of water.

How was whisky tested for proof stength?

Spirit of proof strength was the technical standard by which strength was measured until 1st January, 1980. Hundreds of years ago spirit of this strength was proved when whisky and gunpowder were mixed and ignited. If the gunpowder flashed then there was enough whisky in the mixture to permit ignition. Such whisky was held to have been proved. If the spirit was weaker than this proof strength, ignition did not take place. In the 1740s the Customs and Excise and the London distillers began to use Clark's hydrometer, an instrument devised to measure spirit strength. A more accurate version by Batholomew Sikes was universally adopted under the Hydrometer Act, 1818, and remained in standard use until 1980.

Why is whisky duty-free at sea?

Whisky for consumption on board ships at sea is 'ship's stores',goods taken on board an outward bound ship for officers, crew and passengers during the voyage. The theory is that the stores are in effect exports, in that they are consumed outside U.K. territory, and that the Treasury cannot expect to collect the duty they would bear if consumed at home.

Does Scotch whisky in a bottle lose its strength with age?

Once bottled, whisky does not lose its strength.

Does Scotch whisky improve in a bottle which is kept sealed?

No. There is no change in a whisky once it has been bottled and securely sealed.

At what temperature is whisky best served?

This is a matter of personal choice but room temperature is normal.

Is the bouquet of Scotch whisky improved by warming slightly?

No, this would only increase the rate of evaporation.

What is the best shape of a whisky glass?

No specific shape is required.

What is the measure at which Scotch whisky is sold across the counter?

The Weights and Measures Act of 1963 provides for three standard measures which are one quarter, one fifth and one sixth of a gill equal respectively to one and a quarter fluid ounces, one fluid ounce and five sixths fluid ounce. The proprietor of licensed premises must display a notice in the bar showing which of these quantities he is serving. In Scotland the usual measure is one fifth of a gill and in England one sixth.

CHAPTER SEVEN
Associations
and Heritage Centres

■ The Scotch Whisky Association represents all the principal firms of distillers and blenders (but not retailers) engaged in the Scotch whisky industry and has about 120 members.

It exists to protect and promote the interests of Scotch whisky and the Scotch whisky industry.

The head office is at 20 Atholl Crescent, Edinburgh EH3 8HF. (Tel. 031 229 4383). The address of the London office is 17 Half Moon Street, London W1Y 7RB. (Tel.071 629 4384).

■ The Malt Distillers' Association of Scotland is based at 1 North Street, Elgin, Morayhsire, (Tel. 0343 544077). In general the members of this association are also members of the Scotch Whisky Association.

■ The Scotch Malt Whisky Society was formed in 1983 by a small group of Scots connoisseurs who had discovered the superiority of whisky taken straight from the cask.

In flavour and, of course, in strength, these whiskies are markedly different from the commercially bottled versions which have been chill filtered and diluted.

The Society selects particularly fine casks and bottles the contents without dilution or any intervening process.

Since the whisky from each cask is individual in character, the casks are bottled separately and identified on the label.

The Society's members receive regular newsletters listing the whiskies currently available in bottle.

Orders are then dispatched by insured post to members throughout Britain and abroad.

The Society also holds frequent tastings throughout the country at which members and their guests may sample its wide range of malts.

The Society is based at The Vaults in Leith, the old port of Edinburgh. This is a four-storey wine warehouse built at various dates between the 14th and the 18th centuries.

The Society has a large and splendid 19th century members' lounge and bar, a tasting room, offices, and two small well-appointed flats which are available for members' use.

■ The Scotch Whisky Heritage Centre is based at 354 Castlehill, the Royal Mile, Edinburgh, beside the Castle.

This is a living museum which recreates the history and manufacturing processes of whisky.

There are models, waxworks, audio-visual aids and state-of-the-art devices for bringing the heritage of Scotland's national drink to life.

Guided tours in a selection of languages can be arranged for pre-booked parties.

■ The Speyside Cooperage Visitor Centre is based at Dufftown Road, Craigellachie, Banffshire.

It is a working cooperage and also has a Victorian era museum which has an 'acorn to cask' exhibition.

Each year the cooperage either makes or repairs more than a hundred thousand casks and visitors are welcome to savour the sights, sounds and smells of the bustling workshops.

CHAPTER EIGHT

The Malts

Mᴬⁿʸ Scotch whisky distilleries welcome visitors throughout the year.

Here are the main ones with a brief outline of their products.

For details on when best to visit, a phone call in advance is advised.

Most of the visits are by appointment only. There are also visitors centres at many of them.

ABERLOUR-GLENLIVET,

Aberlour-on-Spey,
Banffshire AB38 9PJ.
September - June
Monday - Thursday 10 a.m. - 4 p.m.
All visits by appointment.
Contact: Distillery Office at 0340 871204.

This is a 12-year-old single malt.

The distillery is set in a romantic setting at the foot of Ben Rinnes where the Lour Burn joins the River Spey.

It was founded in 1879 on the site of an ancient one but has been extensively modernised.

This whisky is smooth and aromatic and should be drunk after a good dinner.

The MASTER of Malt

ABERFELDY

13 years old

SINGLE HIGHLAND MALT WHISKY

Distilled 15th December 1992

Bottled November 1992

A limited edition bottling from cask no. 7789

Established in 1896, this Perthshire distillery is licenced to John Dewar & Sons Ltd. Aberfeldy is the last of several distilleries that once existed in the area. Its water source is the Pitilie Burn.

70cl   Produce of Scotland   43% vol

Bottled exclusively in Scotland for The Master of Malt

ABERFELDY,
Aberfeldy,
Perthshire PH15 2EB.
Easter - October.
Monday - Friday 10 a.m. - 4 p.m.
Group bookings by appointment.
November - March.
By appointment only.
Contact: Distillery office at 0887 820330.

Built in 1896 by the Perth-based blenders John Dewar and Sons, this distillery lies close to the River Tay.

Major rebuilding took place in 1972 with four stills in a new stillhouse.

This whisky is pale and has a smooth, orangey fruitiness.

BALBAIR,

Edderton,

Tain,

Ross-shire 1V19 1LB.

September - June

Monday - Thursday 10 a.m. - Noon, 2 p.m. - 4p.m.

Group bookings, maximum 8.

All visits by appointment only.

Contact: Distillery Office at 086282 273.

This is a five-year-old Highland malt.

Built in 1790 on the site of a distillery founded in 1749, the distillery lies within a quarter of a mile of the Dornoch Firth.

All the local streams provide excellent water running through peat which may explain why this malt is unusually young for a malt.

The flavour is delicate, refreshing, clean, smooth and medium bodied while the colouring is pale.

BEN NEVIS,
Lochy Bridge,
Fort William PH33 6TJ.
All year.
Monday - Friday 9 a.m. - 5 p.m.
July - August 9 a.m. - 7.30 p.m.
Easter - September.
Saturday 10 a.m. - 4 p.m.
Group bookings by appointment - max. 15.
Contact: Visitors centre at 0397 700200.

This was founded by 'Long John' Macdonald in 1825 and a cask was presented to Queen Victoria when she visited Fort William in 1848.

The flavour is medium-sweet, smoky and smooth with a little tannin and a green freshness.

BLAIR ATHOL,
Pitlochry,
Perthshire PH16 5LY.
Easter - October
Monday - Saturday 9.30 a.m. - 4.30 p.m.
also Sunday noon - 4.30 p.m.
Admission charge
Group bookings by appointment.
Contact: Visitors Centre at 0796 472234.

This is an eight-year-old Highland single malt.

The distillery was licensed in 1825 on the site of an older one.

Arthur Bell and Sons bought it in 1933 and the building is set in scenic surroundings with colourful gardens full of rhododendrons and roses in summer.

The flavour is smoky and light and this whisky is excellent as an aperitif.

BOWMORE,
School Street,
Bowmore,
Isle of Islay PA43 7GS.
All year Monday - Friday Tours (10 a.m. - 3.30p.m.)
Group bookings, evening and weekend visits by appointment only.
Contact: Visitors Centre at 049681 671.
  This distillery is one of the oldest in the Hebrides.
  It was founded in 1779.
  It still retains the traditional floor method of malting barley.
  Over a century ago this whisky was sold with the Gaelic motto 'Fioghinn agus Soir' which means 'full and excellent quality'.
  The flavour is smoky, peaty, full-bodied and smooth with an amber colour. Drink preferably with water after dinner.

BRUICHLADDICH,
Bruichladdich,
Isle of Islay PA49 7UN.
All year.
Monday - Friday 10a.m. - 5 p.m.
Tours by appointment.
No group bookings.
Contact: Distillery office at 049685 221.
  This distillery is set on the western shore of Loch Indaal on Islay.
  The name is Gaelic for 'the hill on the shore'.
  It went into production in 1881 and some of the original equipment such as the wash tun brewing tank is still in use.
  It is one of the few Scottish distilleries to have riveted stills.
  The water is some of the best in a country rich in good water and is drawn directly from the heather covered hills.
  The flavour is peaty and smooth and the colour golden.

BUNNAHABHAIN,

Port Askaig,
Isle of Islay PA46 7RP.
All year.
Monday - Friday 10 a.m. - 4p.m.
Group bookings - max.12.
All visits by appointment.
Contact: Distillery office at 049684 646.

This is a twelve-year-old single malt.

The distillery is the most northerly on Islay and was opened in 1883 b
the Greenlees brothers, both local farmers, to make use of their grain.

The name translates as 'mouth of the river' because the building is situ
ated near the mouth of the river Margadale which flows into the Sound c
Islay.

In 1887 the Islay Distillery Company, which had begun building the dis
tillery six years earlier, amalgamated with Glenrothes-Glenlivet to form th
Highland Distilleries Co.

A publication of the 1880s describes how the distillery had been provid
ed with a good road, a handsome pier and a reading room and schoolroor
for the workmen's children.

The sense of community that grew up around the distillery can still b
sensed to this day.

The flavour is lightly peated and delicate with a smooth, well-roundec
mellow flavour. Dark in colour, it can be taken anytime.

ISLAY
SINGLE MALT SCOTCH WHISKY

CAOL ILA

*distillery, built in 1846 is situated near Port Askaig on the Isle of Islay.
Steamers used to call twice a week to collect whisky from this remote
site in a cove facing the Isle of Jura. Water supplies for mashing
come from Loch nam Ban although the sea provides water for
condensing. Unusual for an Islay this single MALT SCOTCH
WHISKY has a fresh aroma and a light yet well rounded flavour.*

AGED 15 YEARS

43% vol .... 70 cl

CAOL ILA,
Port Askaig,
Isle of Islay PA46 7RL.
All year.
All visits by appointment.
Contact: Distillery Office at 049684 207.

The name means 'Sound of Islay' which is the stretch of water that separates the island from Jura.

Lying by the sea, the distillery was acquired by Bulloch Lade in 1857 and extended and improved by them in 1879.

Drawing water from the fragrant Loch Nam Bam which is surrounded by myrtle and heather, this whisky is also an essential ingredient in the 'BL' Gold Label and Old Rarity blends.

The flavour is tangy and peaty.

CARDHU,
Knockando,
Aberlour,
Banffshire AB38 7RY.
All year.
Monday - Friday 9.30 a.m. - 4.30 p.m.
May - September also Satruday 9.30 a.m. - 4.30 p.m.
Admission charge.
Group bookings by appointment.
Contact: Distillery office at 03406 204.

This is a 12-year-old single Highland malt.

The name in Gaelic means 'black rock' and refers to the neighbouring Mannoch Hills which are the source of the distillery's spring water.

Set in a remote Speyside glen, it originated when John Cumming took a lease out on Cardow Farm in 1811 and five years later was convicted on three occasions for distilling without a licence.

His wife did the brewing and his daughter-in-law inherited the business and expanded the premises.

In 1893 John Walker and Sons, who along with other blenders needed to secure a good source of supply, bought the distillery from the Cumming family though a son was retained as distillery manager.

Cardhu remains a key ingredient of the Johnny Walker blends.

The flavour is clean, delicate, smooth and mellow and the colour is pale. Preferably consumed after dinner with or without water.

CLYNELISH,
Brora,
Sutherland KW9 6LR.
Easter - October.
Monday - Friday 9.30 a.m. - 4.30 p.m.
November - March by appointment only.
Group bookings by appointment.
Contact: Distillery office at 0408 621444.

This was established in 1819 by the Marquess of Stafford who had married the heiress of the vast Sutherland estates and took that name when he was made a duke.

He was infamous in the Highland Clearances and a huge statue of him still stands atop Ben Bhraggie. He cleared 15,000 crofters from half a million acres.

The distillery fitted into a plan for regenerating arable land on the coast.

Clynelish Farm was let to a Mr. Harper from the Lowlands who built the distillery in an attempt to provide smaller tenants with a market for their grain apart from illicit distillers.

Grains left over used to feed the farm pigs whose manure was used to reclaim part of the Brora Muir.

Coal from the mine at Brora was used in the distillery furnaces.

The premises were enlarged over the years and in 1925 the Distillers Company acquired all the shares.

It closed during the Depression and the war years but in the 1960s a new distillery was built on an adjacent site. In 1975 the old distillery was reopened as Brora Distillery.

The taste is dry and recommended as an after-dinner drink.

DALMORE,
Alness,
Ross-shire 1V 17 OUT.
Mid August - Mid December and Mid January - Beg. June
Monday - Friday
Tours - 10 a.m. and 2 p.m.
Group bookings - maximum 10.
All visits by appointment.
Contact: Distillery office at 0349 882362.
   This is a ten-year-old Highland single malt.
   The first Dalmore whisky ran into oak casks in 1839.
   Originally there were two stills but now there are eight which produce up
to 14,300 gallons of alcohol each week and there are warehouses for 3.3
million gallons.
   The colour is golden and the taste mellow, full-bodied and lingering.

DALWHINNIE,
Dalwhinnie, Inverness-shire PH19 1AB.
All year.
Monday - Friday 9.30 a.m. - 4.30p.m.
Group bookings by appointment.
Contact: Visitor Centre at 05282 208.
The name means 'meeting place' in Gaelic.
The distillery was built in the 1890s at a crossroads for cattle drovers. It was also an area frequented by whisky smugglers.
The Jacobites were active there during the '45 Rebellion and Prince Charlie's cave is nearby where he is reputed to have hidden after Culloden.
This whisky is excellent as an aperitif.

EDRADOUR,

Pitlochry,

Perthshire PH16 5JP.

March - October.

Monday - Saturday 9.30a.m. - 5 p.m.

November - March.

Shop only: Monday - Saturday 10 a.m. - 4 p.m.

Group bookings - max. 50 by appointment.

Contact: Distillery office at 0796 472095.

Set in idyllic scenery, this is Scotland's smallest distillery whose output is only 600 gallons a week.

It is the last of the once numerous Perthshire farm distilleries and the last actually distilling by hand.

The output is two thousand cases a year, the balance being kept as 'top dressing' principally for the House of Lords blend.

The flavour is smooth and malty with a hint of dryness.

FETTERCAIRN,
Fettercairn,
Laurencekirk,
Kincardineshire AB30 1YB.
May - September.
Monday - Friday 10 a.m. - 4.30 p.m.
Group bookings by appointment.
Contact: Visitors Centre at 0561 340205.

The distillery was built in 1824 in the rich, rolling farmlands of the north east.

This is a fairly rare whisky appreciated by connoisseurs. It is mild and light and not as matured as other brands.

It is excellent as an after dinner repast.

GLENALLACHIE,
Aberlour-on-Spey,
Banffshire AB38 9LR.
September - June.
Monday - Thursday 10 a.m. - 4 p.m.
All visits by appointment.
Contact: Distillery office at 0340 871315.

Nestling at the foot of Ben Rinnes, it has four stills and was temporarily closed before being bought by the French Pernod Ricard group which also owns Aberlour and Edradour.

The flavour is full bodied, lightly peated and slightly sweet.

GLENFARCLAS,
Ballindalloch,
Speyside AB37 9BD.
April - October.
Monday - Friday 9 a.m. - 4.30 p.m.
Also Saturday June - September 10 a.m. - 4 p.m.
November - March
Monday - Friday 10 a.m. - 4 p.m.
Admission charge
Group bookings by appointment.
Contact: Visitors Centre at 0807 500257.

This is a single Highland malt whose age can range from eight to 25-years-old.

This independent, family owned distillery celebrated its 150th anniversary in 1986 and is run by the Grant dynasty.

The name means in Gaelic 'glen of the green grassland' and the site of the present distillery was originally a staging post between cattle, horse and sheep farms and the market in Elgin.

It became a popular drink in the U.S.A. after prohibition was repealed.

The flavour is full bodied, lingering and smooth and the colour is dark.

GLENFIDDICH,

Dufftown,
Banffshire AB55 4DH.
Mid October - Easter
Monday - Friday 9.30 a.m. - 4.30 p.m.
Sunday noon - 4.30 p.m.
Group bookings by appointment.
Contact: Visitors Centre at 0340 820373.

This is the leading Scotch malt whisky.

Its founder was William Grant who was born in 1839, the son of a tailor who was also a veteran of Waterloo.

Grant, after many years in the distilling industry during which he saved every penny, bought old plant at the Cardhu Distillery at Knockando for the knockdown price of £119.

He chose for his new plant the slopes of the Conval Hills using water from the Robbie Dubh burn and utilising the power of the Fiddich River to drive the machinery.

With the help of just a mason and carpenter, Grant, always a frugal man, built his distillery for £700 and began distilling.

The first whisky was produced on Christmas Day 1887 and when Smith's Glenlivet Distillery caught fire Grant was able to step in and meet an order.

The business prospered and in 1892 Grant built a second one at Balvenie.

The whisky is light bodied, smooth, dry, fragrant and fresh and is a distinctive pale colour.

GLENGOYNE,
Dumgoyne near Killearn,
Stirlingshire G63 9LV.
April - November
Monday - Saturday
Tours every hour on the hour 10 a.m. - 4p.m., Saturdays 10 a.m. - 1 p.m.
July - August Tuesday and Thursday, 7 p.m. and 8 p.m.
Wednesdays (April - October) Tour and whisky nosing session - 7.30 p.m.
Booking essential.
December - March.
Visits by appointment only.
Group bookings - max. 50.
Larger parties by appointment.
Contact: Distillery office at 0360 50254.
Admission charge.

Glengoyne distillery is in a wooded glen at the foot of Dumgoyne Hill in the Campsie Hills, Stirlingshire.

Rob Roy was very active in the area round the distillery.

In 1876 Lang Brothers Ltd., the wine and spirit merchants, bought Glengoyne which was further extended and modernized after Lang's was acquired by Robertson and Baxter Ltd.

Glengoyne 10 years old is at the heart of the Lang blends.

The whisky is delicate, sweet, mellow, smooth and medium bodied. The colour is dark.

GLEN GRANT,
Rothes,
Morayshire 1V33 7BS.
Mid-March - September.
Monday - Friday 10 a.m. - 4p.m.
July - August
Monday - Saturday 10 a.m. - 4 p.m.
Group bookings by appointment.
Contact: Distillery Office at 0340 831413.

This distillery was established in Rothes by the brothers James and John Grant who are represented in the 'two Highlanders' label.

The Grants came from a long line of farmers whose living had long since been supplemented by the illicit production of malt whisky.

James Grant became a prominent local businessman and Provost of Elgin.

The business expanded at the turn of the century and it was eventually bought by the Seagram Company in 1978.

The distillery uses water from the Back burn and its eight large 'Grant' stills are coal fired as of old.

This whisky is medium-bodied, malty, smooth and delicate. The colour is pale amber.

THE GLENLIVET,
Ballindalloch,
Banffshire AB37 9DB.
Mid-March - November
Monday - Saturday 10 a.m. - 4 p.m.
July and August
Monday - Saturday 10a.m. - 7 p.m.
Group bookings by appointment.
Contact: Distillery Office at 0807 590427.

There is only one whisky that can call itself THE Glenlivet.

In 1880 the exclusive use of this name was secured by John Gordon Smith after he took legal action against other distillers who had been calling their whisky Glenlivet even although their distilleries were not in the glen. The court ruled that only he could use the label The Glenlivet while ten others could hyphenate their names with Glenlivet.

But The Glenlivet was famous before it was legalised and George 1V was presented with some on his state visit to Scotland in 1822.

The first person to take out a licence under the Excise Act of 1823 was George Smith who built the Glenlivet distillery with the encouragement of his landlord, the Duke of Gordon. His grandfather, John Gow, had changed his name to Smith after fleeing to the area when the Jacobite cause he supported was defeated at Culloden.

His company merged with the Glen Grant Distillery and they became part of the Seagram Company in 1978.

The whisky's colouring is pale amber and the taste is delicate, mellow and malty.

GLENMORANGIE,

Tain,

Ross-shire 1V19 1PZ.

September - June.

All visits by appointment. Max 10.

Tours - Tues/Wed/Thurs. 10.30 a.m. and 2.30 p.m.

Contact: Distillery office at 086289 2043.

The distillery is situated on the shores of the Dornoch Firth near Tain.

The name means 'glen of tranquility'.

The distillery was registered in 1843 but the site by the old farmhouse of Morangie was famous for the production of alcohol since 1738.

The water for the distillery comes from the Tarlogie Springs which flow through sandstone and uses local barley.

The swan-necked stills installed in the 1880s are the highest in the Highlands and ensure that only the purest vapours ascend to the top of the neck column.

The business was purchased by Macdonald and Muir Ltd. in the 1890s and the 16 strong workforce became famous as the Sixteen Men of Tain and are featured individually in the firm's advertising.

It is used in the Highland Queen blend.

The whisky is smoky, delicate, sweet, aromatic, light bodied and smooth and is pale in colour.

GLENTURRET,
The Hosh,
Crieff,
Perthshire PH7 4HA.
January and February.
Monday - Friday 11.30 a.m. - 4.30 p.m. (last tour 2.30 p.m.)
March - December
Monday - Saturday 9.30 a.m. - 6 p.m. (last tour 4.30 p.m.)
Sunday 12 noon - 6 p.m. (last tour 4.30 p.m.)
Group bookings - over 40 preferred.
Admission charge.
Contact: Distillery office at 0764 656565.

This distillery is reputedly the oldest single Highland malt distillery in Scotland.

It was established in 1775 but dates back to 1717 when there were numerous illicit stills in Glenturret all drawing their water from the River Turret.

In 1921 it ceased distilling but James Fairlie bought it in 1957 and began its business revival.

It was producing spirit again by 1960.

Touser, the distillery cat (1963 - 1987) was born in the still house and was reputed the greatest mouser ever - she is on record as having caught 28,899 mice.

The whisky is mellow, full-bodied and smooth. It is very light in colour and usually drunk without water.

GLENDRONACH,

Forgue,
Huntly,
Aberdeenshire AB5 6DB.
September - June.
Monday - Thursday.
Tours: 10 a.m. and 2 p.m.
Group bookings - max. 80.
All visits by appointment only.
Contact: Distillery office at 046682 202.

One of the earliest licensed distilleries in Scotland, its founder, James Allardes, was a frequent guest of the 5th Duke of Gordon who was largely responsible for the Excise Act in 1823.

It straddles the Dronach Burn which supplies the cooling water and is situated among tall trees in which rooks nest that are supposed to bring luck.

The flavour is medium-dry, quite rich, full, smooth with a touch of spice and slightly smoky.

Glenkinchie

LOWLAND SINGLE MALT
SCOTCH WHISKY

Glenkinchie Distillery was established in 1837 by John and George Rate. It is situated beside the Kinchie Burn in the heart of East Lothian farmland. Over the gently rolling hills around Glenkinchie, some of the finest barley is grown.

Glenkinchie Lowland Malt Whisky has a light delicate nose and a fresh clean aroma: the finish is smooth, with a subtle hint of dryness. A truly fine distinctive Single Malt, excellent as a pre-dinner drink.

10

YEARS OLD

75 cl e

DISTILLED AT THE GLENKINCHIE DISTILLERY
PENCAITLAND SCOTLAND

43% vol

GLENKINCHIE,
Pencaitland,
East Lothian EH34 5ET.
All year.
Monday - Friday 9.30 a.m. - 4.30 p.m.
Group bookings by appointment.
Contact: Visitor Centre at 0875 340451.

The distillery has long been involved in things agricultural, managers in past years having won fatstock prizes at Smithfield and Edinburgh, the beasts flourishing on the distillery by-products.

It has a museum of distilling which includes an enormous scale model of a distillery.

The flavour is dry, malty, quite spicy and smooth.

GLEN ORD,
Muir of Ord,
Ross-shire 1V6 7UJ.
All year.
Monday - Friday 9.30 a.m. - 4 p.m.
Admission charge.
Group bookings by appointment.
Contact: Distillery office at 0463 870421.

Built on the site of a smuggler's bothy, it is the last of many distilleries that once flourished in the area.

The flavour is rich and fresh, full and round with a touch of pepperiness.

GLENCADAM,
Brechin,
Angus DD9 7PA.
September - June.
Monday - Thursday 2 p.m. - 4 p.m.
Group bookings - max.10.
All visits by appointment only.
Contact: Distillery office at 03566 22217.

Founded in 1825, the distillery passed through a number of owners until purchased by Hiram Walker in 1954.

It is now part of Allied Lyons and operated by Caledonian Malt Whisky Distillers.

It has two stills and is half a mile from the River Esk, taking its water from springs in the surrounding hills.

The flavour is medium-sweet, spirity and smooth.

HIGHLAND PARK,
Holm Road,
Kirkwall,
Orkney KW15 1SU.
April - October
Monday - Friday 10 a.m. - 4p.m.
June - August
Saturday 10 a.m. - 4 p.m.
November - March
Monday - Friday
Tour at 2 p.m. and 3.30 p.m.
Admission charge with redemption in shop.
Group bookings by appointment.
Contact: Distillery office at 0856 873107.

This is Scotland's most northerly distillery and is sited overlooking Scapa Flow with its historic naval connections.

Magnus Eunson, an infamous local smuggler, operated an illicit still in the area in the 18th century.

The present distillery was established in the 1790s.

The distillery does all its own malting by hand.

Since 1935 it has been owned by the Highland Distilleries Co.

The whisky is smoky, full bodied, aromatic and dry and is best taken with water.

ISLE OF JURA,
Craighouse,
Isle of Jura PA60 7XT.
September - May
Monday - Friday 9 a.m. - 4 p.m.
All visits by appointment.
Contact: Distillery office at 049682 240.

The label features the island's distinctive range known as the Paps of Jura.

Among the island's claims to fame is the fact that it was there that George Orwell wrote Nineteen Eighty Four.

This whisky is delicate, mellow, smooth with a subtle sweetness. It is light in colour and is best after dinner with water.

KNOCKANDO,

Knockando,

Aberlour,

Banffshire AB38 7RP.

All year.

Monday - Friday 10 a.m. - 4 p.m.

No visitor centre.

All visits by appointment only.

Contact: 071 258 5000 or 03406 205.

 Built in 1904, much of the make is used in the J. & B. blend.

 An individual feature of this whisky is that its bottle states both its year of distillation and date of bottling.

 The flavour is medium-dry and round, dry and delicately spicy.

LAGAVULIN,
Port Ellen,
Isle of Islay PA42 7DZ.
All year.
All visits by appointment.
Contact: Distillery office at 0496 2250.

The name means 'the mill in the hollow'.

The distillery was built on the shoreline to facilitate the loading onto ships.

Illicit distilling went on in the area long before William Graham opened the legal distillery.

The whisky is smoky, peaty, mellow and full bodied with a lingering taste.

SINGLE ISLAY MALT
SCOTCH WHISKY

10
Years Old

The most richly flavoured of
all Scotch whiskies
ESTABLISHED
1815

DISTILLED AND BOTTLED IN SCOTLAND BY

D. JOHNSTON & CO., LAPHROAIG, LAPHROAIG DISTILLERY, ISLE OF ISLAY

40% vol   70 cl

LAPHROAIG,
Port Ellen,
Isle of Islay PA42 7DU.
September - June
Monday - Thursday
Tours: 10.30 a.m. and 2 p.m.
All visits by appointment only.
Contact: Distillery office at 0496 2418.
   The name is Gaelic for 'the beautiful hollow by the broad bay'.
   The distillery was opened in 1815 in a bay sheltered by rocky islands.
   This whisky has a peaty, smoky taste which is quite distinctive. It is best
taken neat or with a little water.

LEDAIG

SINGLE MALT
FROM
THE ISLE OF MULL

1974
Vintage

BOTTLED 1992

This rare old single malt whisky
was distilled at the Ledaig Distillery
on the Isle of Mull by
Ledaig Distillery (Tobermory) Ltd

PRODUCE OF SCOTLAND

70cl   43% Vol

LEDAIG,
Tobermory,
Isle of Mull PA75 6NR.
April - May
Tuesday, Wednesday, Thursday 10 a.m. - 4 p.m.
June - September
Monday - Friday 10 a.m. - 4 p.m.
Admission charge.
Group bookings by appointment.
Contact: Distillery office at 0688 2645.
   This is the old name given to the malt now produced as Tobermory by Tobermory Distilleries Ltd.
   This distillery is the only one on the island of Mull.
   This whisky is excellent as an aperitif.

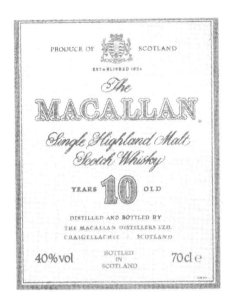

MACALLAN,

Craigellachie,

Banffshire AB38 9RX.

September - June

Monday - Friday

Tours - 11 a.m. and 2 p.m.

July - August restricted visits.

Group bookings - maximum 10 by appointment.

Contact: Distillery at 0340 871471.

This distillery lies in the heart of whisky making territory near the River Spey.

Small copper stills and oak casks that have contained sherry are used for maturing the whisky which is mellow, full bodied and smooth.

MILTONDUFF-GLENLIVET,
Elgin,
Morayshire 1V30 3TQ.
September - June.
Monday - Thursday.
All visits by appointment only.
Contact: Distillery office at 0343 547433.

This distillery forms part of the site of an ancient monastery near Pluscarden Priory on the barley growing plain between Elgin and Forres often referred to as 'the Garden of Scotland'.

According to legend an ancient abbot blessed the waters of the nearby Black Burn and whisky distilled from it was called 'aqua vitae'.

The distillery's old mash house, rebuilt in 1824, was once the brewhouse of the monks.

In 1974 the distillery was extensively modernised and expanded.

This whisky is mellow and full bodied, aromatic with a lingering taste. It is best taken with water.

OBAN,
Oban,
Argyllshire PA34 5NH.
All year.
Monday - Friday 9.30 a.m. - 4.30 p.m.
Easter to October also Saturday 9.30 a.m. - 4.30 p.m.
Admission charge.
Group bookings by appointment.
Contact: Visitor Centre at 0631 64262.

This whisky has the distinction of coming in an unusual bottle with a cork closure.

Situated in the centre of Oban, this distillery predated much of the town which was originally just a small fishing village.

The colour is pale straw with gold highlights and the flavour is smoky and dry with a delicate peatiness.

ROYAL LOCHNAGAR,
Crathie,
Ballater,
Aberdeenshire AB3 5TB.
All year.
Monday - Friday 10 a.m. - 4.30 p.m.
Easter to October also Saturday 10 a.m. - 4.30 p.m. and Sunday 11 a.m. - 4 p.m.
Admission charge.
Group bookings by appointment.
Contact: Distillery office at 03397 42273.

The only remaining distillery on Deeside, this was built in 1845 by John Begg on a site overlooking Balmoral Castle.

It obtained the Royal warrant after Begg invited Queen Victoria and Prince Albert to view the distillery in 1848.

Begg went on to develop the whisky industry by using blends which became world famous under the advertising slogan 'take a peg of John Begg'.

This whisky is sweet and full bodied with a clean taste. The colour is pale with gold highlights.

TALISKER,
Carbost,
Isle of Skye 1V47 8SE.
April - October
Monday - Friday 9.30 a.m. - 4.30 p.m.
November - March by appointment only.
Admission charge.
Group bookings by appointment.
Contact: Distillery office at 0478 640203.
 This is the only distillery on Skye and dates from 1833.
 It lies under Cnoc nan Speireag ('Hawk Hill') in a lonely glen on the west coast of the island.
 This is a pungent, peaty whisky, pale in colour.

TAMDHU,

Knockando,
Aberlour,
Banffshire AB38 7RP.
April - October
Monday - Friday 10 a.m. - 4 p.m.
June - September
Saturday 10 a.m. - 4 p.m.
Group bookings by appointment.
Admission charge with redemption in shop.
Contact: Distillery office at 0340 810486.

Built in 1896, it closed from 1927 until 1947 but was extended in 1972 from two to four stills and again to six stills in 1975.

Sited on the banks of the River Spey, it is the only distillery to malt all its own barley on site.   It gets its water from a spring under the building.

The flavour is round, mellow, sweet and slightly spicy and peaty.

TAMNAVULIN-GLENLIVET,
Tomnavoulin,
Banffshire AB3 9JA.
Two week before Easter - October.
Monday - Saturday 9.30 a.m. - 4.30 p.m.
Group bookings, max. 60. Over 10 by appointment.
Contact: Visitors centre at 0807590 442.

   The name means in Gaelic 'the mill on the hill' and the River Livet flows past the distillery.

   The area is a popular picnic spot.

   The flavour is mature and sweet with a slight flowery edge.

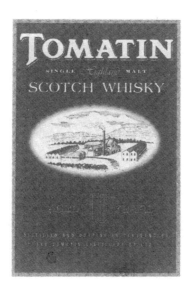

TOMATIN,
Tomatin,
Inverness-shire 1V13 7YT.
All year.
Tours - Monday - Thursday 9 a.m. - noon/2p.m. - 3 p.m.
Friday 2 p.m. only.
Group bookings by appointment.
Contact: Distillery office at 08082 234.
   Built where whisky has been distilled for centuries, it was officially opened in 1897.
   Nearby is The Hill of Parting where the clans disbanded after Culloden.
   Although steeped in history, this distillery is ultra-modern in equipment and is fully automated, making it the biggest producing malt whisky distillery in Scotland.
   Five million proof gallons are produced annually.
   It is also one of the highest distilleries and was the first to be owned by a Japanese company.
   The name in Gaelic means 'the hill of bushes'.
   This whisky is delicate, light bodied and smooth and has a slightly smoky, peaty edge.

TOMINTOUL-GLENLIVET,
Ballindalloch,
Banffshire AB3 9AG.
Mid August - mid December & mid January - beg. June.
Monday - Friday
Tours 10 a.m. & 2 p.m.
Group bookings: max.10.
All visits by appointment only.
Contact: Distillery office at 08073 274.

This is a modern distillery and production only started in 1965 and it was not until 1972 that the make began to appear in bottle.

Built in the highest village in the Highlands, it is frequently cut off by snow in winter.

More than 52,000 litres of alcohol are made there every week and there is warehousing for ten million litres.

This whisky has a lingering, light bodied, smooth taste and is recommended as an after-dinner drink.

TORMORE,
Advie,
Grantown-on-Spey,
Morayshire PH26 3LR.
September - June.
Monday - Thursday 1.30 p.m. - 4 p.m.
Group bookings - max.8.
All visits by appointment only.
Contact: Distillery office at 08075 10244.

Tormore is the first new malt distillery to be erected in the Highlands this century.

It was designed by the architect Sir Albert Richardson to 'blend' into the countryside and came on-stream in 1959.

The workers' houses were designed as part of the overall plan and there is a curling pond and imitation water-mill.

Above the cooperage, a chiming clock strikes up on the hour with the tune 'Highland Laddie'.

This is a smooth, delicate, dry drink.

TULLIBARDINE,
Blackford,
Perthshire PH4 1QG.
September - June.
Monday - Friday 10 a.m. - 4 p.m.
All visits by appointment.
Contact: Distillery Office at 0764682 252.

On the site of an ancient brewery, the distillery takes its name from the nearby moor which is also the site of the Gleneagles Hotel and golf courses.

The area has always been famed for its water.

This whisky is soft, malty and earthy and the flavour is dryish and peppery.

MALT LIQUEUR

Scotland's only malt whisky liquer truly is the spirit of Argyll.

It is a marvellous drink made to a secret recipe of Sandy MacMillan of Tighnabruaich using an eight year old malt complemented with heather highland honey and wild herbs.

Its name is derived from the Island Loch, Melldalloch in Argyll which Sandy owns. This tiny island, with its long history of illicit whisky distilling, had its own ghost called Caileach An Lochan (the old woman of the loch) who was apparently created by the locals to deter unwelcome intruders.

The original "still" is unfortunately in ruins today. However the ghost has not disappeared and was seen as recently as 1979. Legend has it that after a few drams of this fine liqueur you too may see the Old Caileach.

CHAPTER NINE
The Smugglers

IMAGINE Prohibition America of the Roaring Twenties transferred to the Scottish Highlands and you will get a vague idea of the mayhem that was common during the heydays of the whisky smugglers.

They did not have cars or machine guns but the illicit Highland distillers were as adept and violent as any Capone thugs when it came to avoiding the excisemen who were put into the mountains as a Victorian version of the Untouchables.

The whole basis of the problem arose after the Treaty of Union when English revenue staff crossed the border in the vain attempt to bring some fiscal order to the collection of taxes on the thousands of whisky stills smoking quietly away in the Scottish countryside.

Ninety years later the situation was so confused that no two distilleries were taxed at the same rate and illicit distilling flourished.

The Highlander viewed whisky as a gift of the gods and deeply resented having to pay extra revenue for something that literally fell from heaven, certainly as regards one of the main ingredients - water.

Even today an idea of their resentment can be appreciated if you compare the bitter opposition of the Scots to any suggestion that they should pay over the odds for the fluid coming liberally out of their taps.

After a lengthy Royal Commission, the Act of 1823 sanctioned legal distilling at a duty of 2/3 d per gallon for stills with a capacity of more than 40 gallons. There was a licence fee of £10 annually and no stills under the legal limit were allowed.

The first official distillery came into existence in the following year and thereafter many of the more farsighted distillers came over on to the side of the law.

In 1840 the duty was 5d per bottle and the war against the bootleggers began in earnest.

Illicit whisky was not only cheaper but also stronger. Men murdered for it,

Victorian postcard inspired by Burns' famous lampoon of the tax officers - the Deil's awe' wi the exciseman

pitched battles were fought over it and fortunes were made and lost through it.

Entire communities were financially decimated by the war against the smugglers and many households were destroyed by chronic alcoholism.

Smugglers' dens flourished on a massive scale, from bothies in the Borders to caves in the islands.

An illicit still

Fishermen and farmers quit their hard, dangerous trades to participate in the more lucrative black market of illegal whisky.

Government officers were bribed to turn a blind eye and corruption went as high as the judiciary who often quashed court cases, having illegal whisky in their cellars at home.

Some smugglers became so wealthy that they were able to buy large estates.

Various ploys were used to get the product to market. Wives filled pigs' bladders with the liquid and hid these under their dresses. Contents of casks often bore no relation to their labels.

Even funerals were sometimes bogus with whisky being kept in the coffins.

If word came that the excisemen were about to mount a raid, one of the smuggler's family would be pronounced dead from smallpox or some other equally virulently contagious disease thus dissuading them from making house searches.

Since illicit distilling provided the only vent for the disposal of grain over an extensive area of the Highlands, the landed proprietors and gentlemen farmers could hardly be blamed for encouraging it.

Landlords often accepted whisky in payment of rents and it was viewed as a good cure for unemployment and boredom among the more remote crofting areas.

The vigour and perseverance of the smugglers was in striking contrast to the apathy and indifference of the authorities but this changed dramatically when the Government hit on the simple idea of appointing Riding Officers who received bonuses for each sizeable seizure.

But the punishments for illegal distilling had little effect on many miscreants who could notch up a couple of dozen offences over a few years without interrupting their business activities.

Excisemen were killed and wounded - usually by being shot, flung over cliffs or beaten up by mobs - as they went about their duties but getting witnesses and convictions for these offences proved virtually impossible.

Smugglers were sometimes shot dead as they tried to escape excisemen and feelings ran so high in some parts of the Highlands that government officers could not venture into them without the support of troops.

The matter of law and order in the wild Caledonian countryside was raised repeatedly in Parliament with respectable Lowland distillers complaining that their markets were being destroyed by unfair competition to the north.

Fines were increased and the wages of customs men raised.

The Highlanders responded by forming into armed bands, harnessing their sure-footed ponies to traverse the secret mountain tracks to the southern markets.

Glenlivet became the centre of smuggling activity and the whisky trails were busy with convoys of up to thirty men heavy laden with their golden product.

Spies were hired and this led to frequent clashes with the authorities often involving gunfire and swordplay.

Revenue cutters patrolled the coastline, the Caledonian Canal and sea lochs, checking inter-island activity and commandeering smugglers' boats.

Seizures increased as the pressure of legitimate producers improved the efficiency of law enforcement and by the end of last century illegal distilling on a large scale had been effectively stamped out.

Great ingenuity and daring was used to avoid the payment of tax and even today occasional casks get unearthed in unlikely places.

Stills were found under the Free Tron Church in Edinburgh's High Street and under an arch of that city's South Bridge and in a Leith close. Other locations have included next door to the Custom House in Aberdeen,

sheep dips, mountain caverns and underneath many existing distilleries.

The clock tower in the centre of Dufftown once housed a thriving illicit distillery which the local exciseman passed every day on his way to work.

The Loch During smugglers used to attach a cord and small float to their equipment before committing it to the waters of the loch where it could easily be recovered.

At Nigg, Ross-shire, the local smugglers enjoyed the active support of the church beadle who willingly lodged their still in the pulpit in return for a good, regular dram.

But usually the nearest moor or heather-clad hillside offered hiding places galore.

The market for immature, smuggled whisky effectively dried up in the face of plentiful supplies of legally distilled spirits of steadily improving quality and availability.

The attractions of working in a legitimate trade began to look rosier to the natives of the Highlands succumbing to the advances of civilisation than the risky and haphazard ways of the old smuggling life.

By the Edwardian age excise seizures almost entirely involved small isolated stills and the death blow was dealt to the smuggler when the use of barley as a foodstuff became a matter of national security during World War One.

Hysterical alarm about drunkenness among the general population, and ammunition workers in particular, led to much more stringent rules as regards the consumption of alcoholic liquors and any lawbreaking was ruthlessly dealt with as opposed to a measure of leniency prevalent in the past.

Nowadays very few people have the knowledge of how to distil a pleasant spirit so the chances of the colourful days of the whisky smugglers ever returning would seem to be remote.

It was a wild, adventurous time when many of the best qualities of the Scots - initiative, courage, inventiveness - were harnessed to the worst.

CHAPTER 10

The Whisky Still - 1848

*T*HIS *fascinating account of illicit whisky transactions was written and first published by R.R. McIan away back in 1848 in his 'The Highlanders at Home, on the heath, the river and the loch.'*

It is a curious fact that the means of producing artificial excitation, or a pleasing flow of animal spirits, is one of the earliest objects of human solicitude. No sooner have herds been domesticated and the land brought into cultivation, than the invention of man discovers the art of preparing an exhilarating beverage. To the people of the east and the southern countries of Europe, the vine afforded a delicious treat, the want of which the Gauls and Britons supplied from grain, and the liquor prepared from it they named Curmi, a word retained in close resemblance by the Welsh, whose term for beer is Cwrw; the Gaels have lost this word, but they retain Cuirm, a feast, and call ale Loinn, the Llyn, or liquor of the former.

It was reserved for the northern descendants of the Celtic race to improve on the process of fermentation, and by distilling the Brathleis, or wort, they became the noted preparers of Uisge beatha. This term is literally "the water of life", corresponding to Aqua vitae, Eau de vie, &c., and it is from the first portion of the word that 'Whisky' is derived. It is otherwise called Poìt du', or the black pot, in the slang vocabulary of the smuggler, the Irish Poteen, or the little pot, being of similar import.

The superiority of small still spirits to that which is usually produced in large licensed distilleries, is supposed to arise from the more equable coolness of the pipe, a regular supply of spring water being introduced for the condensation of the steam and the Braich, or malt, is also believed to be of a better quality, being made in small quantities, and very carefully attended to. As the preparation of malt for private distillation is illegal, it must be managed with great secrecy, and the writer has seen the process carried on in the Eird houses, often found on the muirs, which, being subterraneous, were very suitable for the manufacture. These rude constructions had been

Making moonshine!

the store-houses for the grain, to be used in another form, of the original inhabitants. Whisky may be sometimes of inferior quality; but where the people are generally so good judges of its worth it is not likely that a bad article will be produced, and it may be observed that the empyreumatic taste, vulgarly called 'peat reek', is a great defect. Tarruing dubailt is double distilled, Treasturruing, three times, and when it is "put four times through," and called Uisge bea'a ba'ol.

From the nature of the traffic, the most secluded spot is selected for the plantation of the simple distillery. Caves in the mountains, coiries or hollows in the upland heaths, and recesses in the glens, are chosen for the purpose, and they are, from fear of detection, often abandoned after the first 'brewst'. The print exhibits a Whisky Still at work in a moonlight night, attended by two gillean, or youths, and the primitive construction of the apparatus is sufficiently made out. Into the tub, or vessel, through which the 'worm', or condensing pipe is conveyed, although not seen in the picture, there is a small rill conducted, which, running through, affords a constant supply of the cold stream.

National as the love of whisky appears to be, it is a matter of doubt whether it has been long known to the Highlanders. Some writers seem to have no doubt that the ancient Caledonians possessed the art of preparing alcohol; but to arrive at the distillation of spirits an acquaintance with chemistry is requisite, and society must be in an advanced state of improvement ere such a manufacture could be attempted. Writers who have directed their attention to the subject, maintain that no satisfactory proof can be found of whisky having been in use at an earlier period than the beginning of the fifteenth century. Certain it is, that malt liquor formed the chief beverage of the old Highlanders, who do not seem to have had so fond a relish for uisge beatha as their successors, and however useful a dram of good Glenlivet may be in a northern climate, it does not appear that the present race are more healthy and hardy than their fathers. General Stewart gives the evidence of a person who died in 1791, at the age of 104, that lionn-laidir, strong ale, was the Highland beverage in his youth, whisky being procured in scanty portions from the low country; yet Prince Charles, at Coireairg, in 1745, elated to hear that Cope had declined battle, ordered whisky for the common soldiers to drink the general's health, which would prove it to have been then plentiful.

Illicit distillation was at one time perseveringly carried on throughout Scotland, and whisky was indeed a staple commodity. Many depended for payment of their rents upon what they could make by this means, and landlords had obvious reasons to wink at the smuggling which prevailed with their knowledge to such an extent among their tenants; some years ago several justices of the peace in Aberdeenshire, were deprived of their commissions, for stating it as impossible to carry into effect the stringent acts passed for the suppression of the illegal practice.

In the fastnesses of the Highland districts it was difficult to discover the bothies, where the work was carried on, and prudence often forbade the gauger from attempting a seizure; but in more accessible parts of the country, his keen search could only be evaded by the utmost vigilance. In Strathdon, Strathspey, and neighbouring localities, where a mutual bond of protection exists, it is the practice, when the exciseman is seen approaching, to display immediately from the house-top, or a conspicuous eminence, a white sheet, which being seen by the people of the next 'town', or farm steading, a similar signal is hoisted, and thus the alarm passes rapidly up the glen, and before the officer can reach the transgressors of the law, everything has been carefully removed and so well concealed, that even when positive information has been given it frequently happens that no trace of the work can be found.

The life of a smuggler is harassing, and the system has a demoralising tendency; from the time he commences malting he is full of anxiety, and the risk he runs of having the proceeds of his painful labour captured in its transit to the customer is not the least of his troubles. Sometimes the low-country people will meet the Highlanders, and purchase the article at their own risk; but it is generally taken by the latter to the towns, and they travel frequently in bodies with horses and carts. Information is often obtained of these expeditions, and the exciseman intercepts it, taking, if necessary, a party of soldiers; but sometimes, after a severe encounter, the smugglers have got off, carrying back a portion of the spirits, and mayhap, leaving wounded or dead on both sides. When the party reaches the vicinity of a town the greatest caution must be observed in going about with the sample of "the dew", and all sorts of expedients are adopted to convey it, when sold, to the premises of the buyer.

CHAPTER ELEVEN
Whisky Galore!

THE Ealing comedy classic 'Whisky Galore', made in 1948, continues to delight new audiences through its video release and repeats on television.

But what few people realise is that the film was based on fact.

During a storm in February, 1941, a freighter, the S.S. Politician, ran aground on rocks off Eriskay.

On board were more than 50,000 cases of whisky en route for the United States at a time when, due to wartime restrictions, it was in short supply at home.

Local islanders proceeded to 'salvage' much of the whisky for their own use before customs men could frustrate them.

Best-selling author Compton Mackenzie, in charge of Barra Home Guard at the time, used the incident as the basis of his most famous novel which in turn was filmed during the summer of 1948.

The producer was Monja Danischewsky, a flamboyant Russian Jew, keen to film on location, who gambled on Alexander Mackendrick, an enthusiastic newcomer, as his director.

The actors and camera crew, numbering over a hundred, flew to Barra for the filming and stayed fourteen rainswept weeks in what was the worst summer for years.

There were precious few beds at the Castlebay Hotel and most of the cast and technicians were billeted on islanders.

This gave their work and performances an additional flavour as they were able to study mannerisms and accents.

In addition, many islanders were used as extras.

Mackendrick was paid £35 a week for his efforts in creating what was to become Scotland's most famous film.

The tension between director and producer created a dramatic contrast in the film.

Mackendrick, strictly brought up by his grandparents in Hillhead, Glasgow, took the side of the island's 'colonial governor' Captain Waggett, with his pendantic obsession about the rule of law, while Danischewsky, anarchic and bohemian, was wholly on ths side of the outrageous locals pillaging to their hearts content.

Waggett was played by the cinema's edifice of English bureaucracy, Basil Radford, who gave a touch of much needed pathos to the role, yet Mackendrick later remarked, "Waggett the Englishman is the most Scottish character in the film. He is the only Calvinist, puritan figure who is against looting. And all the other characters aren't Scots at all - they're Irish."

Compton Mackenzie made a brief appearance as the ship's captain whose most memorable lines in a thick fog were that his ship was nowhere near the rock (this just before the wreck) while other parts went to Joan Greenwood, James Robertson-Justice, Gordon Jackson and Gordon Macrae.

The film teemed with invention and memorable scenes: the fleet of little boats rescuing the cargo; the figures of islanders milling in the midnight streets as the clock chimes announce the end of the sabbath and the resumption of the looting; the celebratory ceilidh; the customs men prowling like the Gestapo; the multifarious ways of hiding bottles of whisky; Captain Waggett baffled and bewildered by it all; the final hectic chase across the sand dunes and the Captain's humiliation to gales of ghostly laughter.

The theme of humanitarian values against the stupid, faceless men in charge struck a chord with post-war audiences still suffering under rationing and familiar with ways of getting 'necessities' by hook or by crook.

'Whisky Galore' was released by Ealing in the same year as their 'Kind Hearts and Coronets' and 'Passport to Pimlico' and was instrumental in linking that studio with the words 'comedy classics'.

It was the studio's most successful film financially and in America was a surprise box-office hit, something not usual for British films, even although its name had to be changed to 'Tight Little Island' because the strict Hays Code forbade overt references to liquor in movie titles.

It was also a smash hit in France, the first time an Ealing film had caught on there.

The Scotch whisky industry was slow to realise the film could be an unofficial advert for their wares but at the Paris premiere they packed the foyer with crates of the best malt like a full ship's hold, an evening which prompted Compton Mackenzie, who attended, to remark, "It was the nearest thing to a Bacchic revel imaginable in the twentieth century."

In France the title was 'Whisky A Gogo' and that soon became the in-name for numerous bars and nightclubs all over the country.

There was a sorry sequel to the film. It was produced in 1958 and called 'Rockets Galore' but it had none of the sparkle of the original.

Mackendrick went on to make other fine films, the best for Ealing being 'The Man In The White Suit', 'The Maggie' and 'The Ladykillers'.

But his first youthful success as a director has never been surpassed as a joyful, exciting, comic slice of one particularly exuberant period of Scottish life.

To return to the facts behind the film:-

The S.S. 'Politician' was a 450 ft., 8000 ton cargo vessel owned by the Harrison Company.

When she grounded in a severe gale she was bound from Liverpool to New Orleans and was heading up through the Minch off the treacherous west coast of Scotland towards Cape Wrath where she was to join a convoy and be escorted across the Atlantic.

Apart from the whisky, her holds were jammed with fur coats, perfumes, cigarettes, cosmetics and bicycles as well as £3 million in brand new currency.

The crew of 52, captained by Beaconsfield Worthington, a Liverpudlian with 40 years experience at sea, were sailing without lights, the normal practice in wartime and navigating on a standard magnetic compass and, as shore and other navigation lights would also be blacked out, the passage up the Minch, often treacherous at the best of times, was especially so for a large, deep sea ship with no radar and no echo sounder.

'By guess and by God' seemed to be the order of the watch and what made the situation even more hazardous was the magnetic pull of some rocks off Eriskay which could make what navigational aids there were go haywire.

She was hit by a Force 9 gale and was driven onto a reef in the pre-dawn darkness off the north tip of Eriskay (which is different from the film where the shipwreck happened in a thick fog).

Her S.O.S. signals were picked up by the Coastguard and Royal Navy and the lifeboat was launched from Castlebay on Barra fifteen miles to the south.

The crew were successfully rescued and under the influence of the islanders' hospitality revealed exactly what still lay aboard their wrecked ship.

By the time the Excisemen, police reinforcements, home guard and salvage experts arrived, the islanders from all over the Hebrides had been raiding the wreck for months, the first buccaneers having gone aboard on the night the ship was officially abandoned.

The first organised raid was hatched on the spur of the moment by two islanders from South Uist.

Seamus Campbell, then 28, was home on leave after his own ship had been torpedoed and had followed the drama with intense interest.

He commandeered his father's fishing boat with neighbour Ronald MacDonald and set sail for the stricken ship.

He later recalled, "It was nearly midnight by the time we reached her and there was a terrible wind blowing. At first there seemed no way on board since the crew had made her secure. We were about to admit defeat when I decided I would climb up the mast of my own boat. The night was black and the boat was tossing about in the storm. I made a leap for the railing and managed to haul myself on board. I threw a rope down to Ronald and he came on board too."

The first drop of whisky to pass their salt-parched lips, he remembers fondly, was from a bottle labelled 'Strathspey'.

But all of it in all its gloriously different and evocative brand names - Highland Nectar, Montain Dew, Black Label, Ballantine's Amber, Haig's Dimple and so on - was thereafter nicknamed as the legendary 'Polly'.

The pair, greeted on their heroic return that night, had thirty cases between them.

That haul was only a drop in the bucket to the 200 cases Seamus had on board when his luck ran out on a later expedition. He got caught and the excisemen put him behind bars in a mainland prison.

Before the 'Politician' was abandoned, the government, recognising that a vast amount of whisky was also being left behind, decided it ought to be protected forever after behind the majestic Seal of H.M. Customs and Excise.

This was duly imprinted on the hatch covers of No. 5 hold and the warning token reinforced with locking bars.

Motor boat patrols round-the-clock would have been the only real deterrent but such resources simply were not available to the lcoal excisemen and constabulary who could not even stretch to putting nightwatchmen aboard.

Meanwhile, the pillaging contiued apace.

Just how fast the whisky was consumed is indicated by Seamus Campbell referring to his 'maiden voyage', "We promised ourselves we would not be too greedy and we would try to make the whisky last until Christmas. But it was all gone by the end of the week so we went back for more."

The pitch black of the cavernous whisky hold was partially dispelled by the eerie light from dozens of guttering candles and tilly lamps and scores of whispering shadows bent to their tasks as if worhipping a midnight mass in a cathedral.

Close up, the devil himself might have dived over the side at the sight of some of the raiders.

Most were as black as Old Nick himself, covered from head to toe in fuel oil and festooned in makeshift plaids of garish silks and cottons to keep their own clothes as clean as possible.

The decks were covered in slippery oil and men struggling to the rails under a burden of cases often ended up sliding on their beam ends and screeching curses after tripping over stray ropes and abandoned knick-kncaks from less profitable packages.

The recovery of the cases themselves required something of an acquired skill involving the use of a home-made tool like a spear with a barb for hooking under the wire of the boxes in the inky darkness of the flooded hold.

Bearing in mind the hold was about a hundred feet long and 50 broad and the deck towered 50 feet above the waterline there was obviously a lot of crawling to be done from the crowded vantage points closest to the slimy surface.

Once the cases were hooked, they would be tied on to the end of, usually, a roll of finest cloth and hauled the rest of the way up to the top deck.

At times the ship had the appearance of a Royal yacht, bedecked as she was with fluttering pennants of brightly coloured discarded silks and cottons.

On the deck groups would be exchanging pleasantries and news from different townships and islands, friendships made and renewed as unbroken circles of bottles passed from hand to hand and mouth to mouth. Choruses in Gaelic would start up as well as the mouth music and some impromptu Highland dancing.

At this time, little old ladies, perhaps too stiff of a winter's morning with the athritis to get down on their knees and puff the embers of the peat fire into flame, began to see other magical properties in the deluge of alcohol.

A son arriving home on leave at his mother's house on Eriskay could scarcely believe the tales of the abandoned whisky.

Striding in the door his soul soared aloft when he spotted, uncorked on the mantelpiece, a three quarter full bottle of King George V.

He got his fist round the neck but before he got it halfway to his face his mother bounded out of the bedroom screeching, "Don't drink the Geordie, for God's sake."

"Why's that for, mother?" he asked, alarmed.

"Because it's for lighting the damned fire. It's no' so tasty as the rest."

The finest whiskies in the world out of the hands of drinking men became quite a domestic necessity for the housewives of many homes in the place of disinfectants, unguents against sheep tick and flea bites, and medicines for cattle and babies.

In those early days it was like a harvest with no end and not a cloud in the sky.

Those who went to confession, as most of the immediate islanders were Catholic, might have expressed sincere guilt at getting blind, blazing drunk and beating the wife or even a pal.

But the sin of thievery was never on their conscience.

The unwritten code of centuries was clear.

Once a ship was abandoned, she was the property of nobody - but anyone who cared to lighten her load.

However, now the revenue men began to get anonymous tips that such and such a crofter was hoarding whisky, presumably from a minority of aggrieved neighbours who felt they were getting an insufficient slice of the action or who were too scared to take part.

Convictions began to mount up at the court in Lochmaddy.

The first four accused, from Barra, were fined a total of £13 for the illegal possession of whisky.

A string of others sailed up the Minch for trial and sentence and one of them was jailed for six weeks while another six from Uist got two months and another a month.

A total of 40 cases were dealt with and 13 received prison sentences.

The days of whisky galore were gone forever and the islanders returned to their more mundane tasks.

92